Poems Out Loud

Selected by Brian Moses

HODDER
Wayland

an imprint of Hodder Children's Books

10 9 8 7 6 5 4 3 2

A catalogue record for this book is available from the
British Library

Designer: Jane Hawkins

ISBN: 0340 89401 6

Printed and bound in Great Britain by Bookmarque Ltd,
Croydon, Surrey

The Paper and board used in this paperback are natural
recyclable products made from wood grown in sustainable
forests. The manufacturing processes conform to the
environmental regulations of the country of origin.

Hodder Children's Books
A division of Hodder Headline Limited
338 Euston Road, London NW1 3BH

Introduction

Poetry has been composed and performed since earliest times. Before poems were written down they were chanted and sung, they were danced and set to music, and today, it is when printed poems leave the page that they really come to life.

As you read 'Poems Out Loud' and listen to the accompanying CD, you will find a wide selection of poetry, both traditional and modern. There are poems with percussion, poems with prerecorded backing tracks, poems with choral speaking, poems shouted, poems sung and poems whispered. Hopefully the one thing that links all these poems together – their rhythms – will be clearly evident from what you read or hear.

Such oral poetry however, is never set in stone. It changes with each new interpretation. Poems grow as they are performed over the years, and the words that you read on the printed page may differ slightly to those spoken by the poets.

And once you've read or heard the poems, why not add your own interpretation? Shout, sing, dance, play a drum – these are performance poems. Try them out.

Brian Moses

Contents

Mega Star Rap

I'm king of the keyboard, star of the screen,
They call me Gamesmaster, you know what
   I mean,
'Cause I am just ace on the Nintendo action,
When I get in my stride, you know, I don't give
   a fraction,
With Super Mario I'm a real daredevil,
I'm cool, I'm wicked, on a different level!
I'll take on anyone who wants to challenge me,
No matter what the problem is, I hold the key.
I can tell you every shortcut on the Megadrive,
I can put the Sonic Hedgehog into overdrive,
And I would, I really would like to accept
   your dare,
But I've just run out of batteries for my Sega
   Game Gear.

   Valerie Bloom

Bears Don't Like Bananas

Monkeys like to play the drums,
  badgers wear bandannas.
Tigers like to tickle toes
  but bears don't like bananas.

A crocodile can juggle buns
  on visits to his Nana's.
Seagulls like to dance and sing
  but bears don't like bananas.

Rats and mice can somersault
  and do gymnastics with iguanas.
Weasels like to wiggle legs
  but bears don't like bananas.

A porcupine likes drinking tea
  and cheering at gymkhanas.
A ladybird likes eating pies
  but bears don't like bananas.

John Rice

Keeping Fit

Forget aerobics and gymnastics.
I'm keeping fit with mathematics.
None of this jogging lark
and malarky round the park.

I burn up calories
swivelling my shoulder
three hundred and sixty degrees.
I become a circle
turning on two bent knees.

Now it's doubles and trebles
with toes and knuckles.
I multiply inbreath
by outbreath.
That usually works up a sweat.

Now watch me extend my arms
into parallelograms.
With a twist of the torso
I squat like a zero.
Then to test my flexibility
I stretch and s t r e t c h and s t r e t c h
to infinity.

John Agard

He Just Can't Kick It With His Foot

John Luke from our team
Is a goalscoring machine
Phenomenally mesmerising but ...
The sport is called football
But his boots don't play at all
   Cos he just can't kick it with his foot.

He can skim it from his shin
He can spin it on his chin
He can nod it in the net with his nut,
He can blow it with his lips
Or skip it off his hips
   But he just can't kick it with his foot.

With simplicity and ease
He can use his knobbly knees
To blast it past the keeper, both eyes shut,
He can whip and flick it
Up with his tongue and lick it
   But he still can't kick it with his foot.

Overshadowing the best
With the power from his chest
Like a rocket from a socket he can put,
The ball into the sack
With a scorcher from his back
    But he just can't kick it with his foot.

Baffling belief
With the ball between his teeth
He can dribble his way out of any rut,
Hypnotise it with his eyes
Keep it up on both his thighs
    But he just can't kick it with his foot.

From his shoulder to his nose
He can juggle it and pose
With precision and incision he can cut,
Defences straight in half
With a volley from his calf
    But he just can't kick it with his foot.

He can keep it off the deck
Bounce the ball upon his neck
With his ball control you should see him strut,
He can flap it with both ears
To loud applause and cheers
   But he just can't kick it with his foot.

He can trap it with his tum
Direct it with his bum
Deflect it just by wobbling his gut,
When he's feeling silly
He can even use his ankle
But he just can't kick, he just can't kick,
He can pick it up and flick it
Do every type of trick
   But he just can't kick it with his foot.

Paul Cookson

Mum

She's a:

Sadness stealer.
Cut-knee healer.
Hug-me-tighter.
Wrongness righter.
Gold-star carer.
Chocolate sharer
(well sometimes!).

Hamster feeder.
Bedtime reader.
Great game player.
Night-fear slayer.
Treat dispenser.
Naughty sensor
(how come she always knows?).

She's my
Never-glum,
Constant-chum,
Second-to-none,
(We're under her thumb!)
Mum!

Dad

He's a:

Tall-story weaver.
Full-of-fib fever.
Bad-joke teller.
Ten-decibel yeller.
Baggy-clothes wearer.
Pocket-money bearer.
Nightmare banisher.
Hurt-heart vanisher . . .

Bear hugger.
Biscuit mugger.
Worry squasher.
Noisy nosher.
Lawn mower.
Smile sower . . .

Football mad.
Fashion sad.
Not half bad.
So glad I had
My
Dad!

Andrew Fusek Peters and Polly Peters

My Mum's Sari

I love my mother's sari on the washing line
Flapping like a giant flag, which I pretend is mine.

I love it's silky softness when it's folded to a square
Which I can roll into a ball and pretend it isn't there.

I love to hold its free bit that swings over
   mum's back
And wrap it round my shoulders, like a potato
   in a sack.

I love the pleats that fall in shape and spread out
   like a fan
Where my kid brother crouches and says
   'catch me if you can'.

I love to wash my dirty hands at the kitchen sink
And wipe them on mum's sari before she can
   even blink.

But when she takes her anchal and ties it round her
   waist
I know its time for battle and a quick escape
   is best!

Bashabi Fraser

I'm Not a Kid

I'm not a kid, ok
I'm not a kid, I say
I'm not a kid.

Kids have horns,
Kids go ma-ay,
Kids live with goats,
And anyway

Kids don't wear trousers,
Don't wear shirts,
Kids don't eat lemon pies
For dessert.

So I'm not a kid, ok
I'm not a kid, I say
I'm not a kid.

Don't call me a kid
'Cause I don't like it,
Don't call me a kid, I'm a
Child, don't fight it.

Kids have hooves,
Kids chew the cud,
Kids nibble grass,
Kids eat rose buds.

So I'm not a kid, ok
I'm not a kid, I say
I'm not a kid.

Kids are animals
like a gnu,
A cow, a giraffe,
Or a kangaroo.

I don't have four feet,
Not covered with hair,
Can you see a tail on me?
Anywhere?

'Cause, I'm not a kid, ok
I'm not a kid, I say
I'm not a kid.

Oh, look, Mum,
Look over there,
See, 'Flights to Eurodisney,
Extra low fare.'

Can we go, please, Mum?
No need to pay for me,
See, that sign there says
"Kids Go Free!"

Valerie Bloom

The Cat with No Name

It was drizzly December when the cat first
 appeared
and took the French teacher's chair for
 his bed.
Now his scimitar claws in the staffroom
 are feared,
oh yes, and the street-fighter's teeth in
 his head.
Once a day he is seen doing arches and
 stretches,
then four hours like a furry coiled fossil
 will lie.
It's true that he's made all the staff nervous
 wretches.
They approach . . . and he opens one
 basilisk eye.

For the teachers
know very well not to stroke him.
They know that he won't play the game.
He's a wild cat,
a not-to-be-riled cat.
He's a tortoiseshell cat with no name.

I once worked in that school and observed
    the huge creature's
habits as I sipped my cracked cup of weak
    tea.
I saw how he frightened and flummoxed the
    teachers,
and how – every Friday – he'd one-green-eye
    me.
To appease him, each day we laid out a fish
    dinner
which the beast snaffled-up in just one
    minute flat
then returned to his chair with a smirk – the
    bad sinner!
It seems there's no way to be rid of that cat.

For the teachers
know very well not to cross him.
They know that he's three parts not tame.
He's a wild cat,
a wild cat,
a not-to-be-riled cat.
(He can't bear to be smiled at).
He's the tortoiseshell cat with no name,
with no name.
He's the tortoiseshell cat with no name.

Wes Magee

Cool Cat

Well I'm a cat with nine
And I'm in my prime
I'm a Casanova Cat
And I'm feline fine
I'm strolling down the street
In my white slipper feet
Yeh, all the little lady cats
Are looking for a treat
Because I got style
I got a naughty smile
I'm gonna cross this street
In just a little while
   to be with you
   to be with you
   to be with you
   to be with
You got grace
You got a lickable face
I'm gonna love ya and leave ya
And you'll never find a trace

Because I'm on my own
I like to be alone
I'm just a swingin', strollin',
Rollin' stone
But it's your lucky day
I'm gonna pass your way
I can spare a little lovin'
If you wanna stop and
   play with me
   play with me
   play with me
   play with
Meeow my
I got a twinkling eye
I'm gonna cross this street
So don't you be too shy
But what's this I see
Comin' straight at me
It's a crazy car driver
Tryin' to make me flee

So I look up slow
Just to let the man know
That I don't go any faster
Than I really wannna . . .

X ! X ! X ! X ! X ! X !

Well I'm a cat with eight
I guess he couldn't wait
But I'm looking good
And I'm feline great!

Mike Jubb

The Tyger

Tyger! Tyger! burning bright
In the forests of the night,
What immortal hand or eye
Could frame thy fearful symmetry?

In what distant deeps or skies
Burnt the fire of thine eyes?
On what wings dare he aspire?
What the hand dare seize the fire?

And what shoulder, and what art
Could twist the sinews of thy heart?
And, when thy heart began to beat,
What dread hand? and what dread feet?

What the hammer? what the chain?
In what furnace was thy brain?
What the anvil? what dread grasp
Dare its deadly terrors clasp?

When the stars threw down their spears,
And water'd heaven with their tears,
Did he smile his work to see?
Did he who made the lamb make thee?

Tyger! Tyger! burning bright
In the forests of the night,
What immortal hand or eye
Dare frame thy fearful symmetry?

William Blake

The Monkey

Monkey, monkey, swinging high
In the treetops in the sky,
Are we brothers, are we one,
All together in the sun?

Who gave you that frame so frail?
Who made you that curling tail?
Why have you such puffy cheeks?
Why such scratches and such shrieks?

Do you wonder why the fuss?
Do you give a thought to us?
Funny, cute and somewhat queer,
Warm and furry, full of cheer.

When you leap from tree to tree,
Are you glad that you are free?
You are nimble, you are quick,
You are up to every trick.

Human hands mark you our kin.
Monkey mischief makes us grin.
If I could I would erase
All the sadness from your gaze.

Monkey, monkey, swinging high
In the treetops in the sky,
We are brothers, everyone,
All together in the sun.

Debjani Chatterjee

This poem is a parody of
William Blake's famous 'The Tyger'.

The Wolf's Wife Speaks

He was always out and about.
First on the block
To be up at the crack of dawn
Sniffing the morning air.

Of course,
Pork was his favourite.
I tell you, he would go a long way
For nice bit of crackling,
Or to catch a tasty piglet or two.

But in the end
It all got too much –
All that huffing and puffing
Up and down the den,
Muttering in his sleep
That he would blow the house down!

Something was wrong,
I could tell –
Some thing had put his nose
Out of joint.

He'd come home full of bravado,
Swaggering into the den,
Flashing me that wolfish grin –
All teeth and tongue –
Then he'd set about boasting,
Full of big talk about
blowing up another building.
It cut no ice with me.

The tell-tale signs were there –
Some days he'd get back
covered in straw,
hardly able to draw breath.
What he'd been up,
Lord alone knows...

Well it all came to a head,
When late one afternoon –
He shot back in,
With his fur singed.

I had to laugh –
He looked so funny,
Stood there with his bare bottom
Red as a radish.
Talk about coming home
With his tail between his legs!
Where he'd been – I can't imagine.
He never said.

He stays more at home now.
Well, he's prone to bronchitis –
This time of year you can hear him coming,
Poor old thing –
Wheezing and puffing,
Hardly able to draw breath.

We don't talk about it –
And he's right off pork!
If you ask me,
Its all been
a bit of a blow
To his ego.

Pie Corbett

Aching Bones

There's nothing badder
than an adder
with aching bones.
He moans and groans,
and hisses and bites
and gets into fights,
over nothing.
So something
has to be done for the adder
or he gets badder and madder.
But teach him some yoga,
he'll sway like a cobra;
tying himself in knots,
he'll think sweet thoughts.
There's nothing gladder
than an adder
who owns
flexible bones.

Debjani Chatterjee

The Sssnake Hotel

An Indian python will welcome you
to the Sssnake hotel.
As he finds your keys he'll maybe enquire
if you're feeling well.
And he'll say that he hopes
you survive the night,
that you sleep without screaming
and don't die of fright
at the Sssnake hotel.

There's an anaconda that likes to wander
the corridors at night,
and a boa that will lower itself onto guests
as they search for the light.
And if, by chance, you lie awake
and nearby something hisses,
I warn you now, you're about to be covered
with tiny vipery kisses,
at the Sssnake hotel.

And should you hear a chorus of groans
coming from the room next door,
and the python cracking someone's bones,
please don't go out and explore.
Just ignore all the screams
and the strangled yells
when you spend a weekend
at the S^ss_snake hotel.

Brian Moses

Use Your Rains

The raindrops, are quietly gathered in the stalls
now, thundering hooves, pawing the ground,
anxious for the start, at the 7.45 from Sundown.
The gun goes off like lightning, And they're off,
leaping the first fence in a bunch, they land in
the mud with a splash; the crowd of crows go
wild, as Bit-OF-A-Drip surges into the lead.
Close behind is Storm-Sausage, who is on
sizzling good form. But, but, I don't believe it!
Cats'n'Dogs comes bucketing down, Their
owner, Lobelia Completely-Barking is jumping
up and down, cheering her horse on. It's neck
and neck, the wind is screaming in their ears, at
the last hurdle, the dreadful umbrella jump,
impossible, incredible, Cloud-Cuckoo-Land drifts
into the lead, and Rain-In-The-Neck is down and
it's Bit-Of-A-Drip, with Home-Sleet-Home, but in
at the finish by the seat of his pants, at a
hundred-to-sun, it's Soaking-Wetbum!

Andrew Fusek Peters

Electric Guitars

I like electric guitars:
played mellow and moody
frantic or fast –
on CDs or tapes,
at home or in cars –
live in the streets,
at gigs or in bars.
I like electric guitars:
played choppy like reggae
or angry like rock
or chirpy like jazz
or strummy like pop
or heavy like metal –
it bothers me not.
I like electric guitars:
their strings and their straps
and their wild wammy bars –
their jangling and twanging
and funky wah-wahs –
their fuzz boxes, frets
and multi-effects –

pick ups, machine heads,
mahogany necks –
their plectrums, their wires,
and big amplifiers.
I like electric guitars:
played loudly, politely –
dully or brightly –
daily or nightly –
badly or nicely.
I like electric guitars:
bass, lead and rhythm –
I basically dig 'em –
I like electric guitars

James Carter

I like electric guitars:
played mellow or moody,
frantic or fast – on CDs
or tapes, at home or in
cars – live in the streets,
at gigs or in bars.
I like
electric
guitars:
played
choppy
like
reggae
or angry
like
rock or
chirpy
like
jazz or
strummy
like
pop or
heavy
like
metal – it
bothers me not.
I like electric guitars:
their strings and their straps
and their wild wammy bars – their
jangling and twanging and funky
wah-wahs – their fuzz boxes,
frets and multi-effects –
pick-ups, machine
heads, mahogany necks
– their plectrums, their wires,
and big amplifiers. I like electric
guitars: played loudly, politely – dully
or brightly – daily or nightly – badly
or nicely. I like electric guitars:
bass, lead and rhythm –
I basically dig 'em–
I like electric
guitars.

Duppy Jamboree

'Back to back, belly to belly
Ah don't care at all
For me done dead a'ready.
Back to back, belly to belly
In de duppy jamboree.'

What that noise me hearing
Coming from out o' doah?
Mi get out o' bed, pull back de curtain
An peep out tru de window.

Me rub me yeye an look again,
Can't believe wha me just see,
Twenty-seven duppy dere
Staring back at me!

One o' dem stand up dere
With him head under him arm,
One o' dem is a big ole bull
Like de one pon Granpa farm.

But this one yeye dem full o' fire,
And it have on one big ole chain,
Is a rollin–calf! Me shet me yeye,
Den open dem again

When me hear dem singing.
Me open me yeye wide
Ah think one have a horse head
Growing from him side!

De Devil out deh with dem
With him cow–foot an him horn,
Him long tail wrap right roun him wais'
Him pitchfork in him han.

Lawd, him looking up at me!
Him see me! Him a grin!
It look like sey him come
To punish me for all me sin.

Dem comin to de doorway,
Me noh ready yet fe dead!
Me fly into me mama room
An jump into her bed.

Yeye-water runnin dung me face
Till me can hardly see,
'De duppy dem out o' doah, Mama
Doan mek dem come ketch me!'

Mama hold me tight an laugh,
'Noh mek dem frighten you,
Is not a duppy jamboree,
Is just de Jonkunnu.'

Valerie Bloom

'Duppy' is the West Indian name for ghost.

The Witch's Brew

Hubble bubble at the double
Cooking pot stir up some trouble.

Into my pot
there now must go,
leg of lamb
and green frog's toe,

old men's socks,
and dirty jeans,
a rotten egg
and cold baked beans.

Hubble bubble at the double
Cooking pot stir up some trouble.

One dead fly
and a wild wasp's sting,
the eye of a sheep
and the heart of a king,

a stolen jewel
and mouldy salt,
and for good flavour
a jar of malt.

Hubble bubble at the double
Cooking pot stir up some trouble.

Wing of bird
and head of mouse,
screams and howls
from The Haunted House,

and don't forget
the jug of blood,
or the sardine tin
and the clod of mud.

Hubble bubble at the double
Cooking pot stir up some trouble.

Hubble bubble at the double
Cooking pot stir up some trouble.
Hubble bubble at the double
Cooking pot stir up some trouble.

Wes Magee

Casting a Spell on Old Charlie Bell

Now I'll cast many a spell on old Charlie Bell
'cos he didn't play fair and he cheated.
And although I'm a sport from the Kings'
    own court
these spells will be overheated.

By the hem of his coat may he fall from his boat
and get eaten by forty fishes.
May he take a new job to make a few bob
and end up washing the dishes.

May he fall downstairs and be eaten by bears
when he wakes on Friday morning.
Let him slip on an eel, become a
    crocodiles' meal
without a word of warning.

May his bed become soggy and his carpets
   all boggy
when a flood pours over his floor.
May he never be warm and a hurricane storm
blow a tree right through his door.

By the sole of his shoe may a huge kangaroo
chase him miles across the outback.
May a bat bite his toes and a rat steal his nose
and never ever give his snout back.

May every bad goblin from here to old Dublin
plague him in sleep or awake.
May he work in all weathers, be tickled
   by feathers
and his eyeballs baked in a cake.

May a ghost from a grave give his head a
   close shave
and throw all his hair in the ocean.
And may an old banshee from the town of
   Dundee
feed him a poisonous potion.

May a troop of red ants creep into his pants
and cause him to scream and scratch.
May a firework rocket go off in his pocket
next time he lights a match.

May he shake and shiver when he falls in
   the river
and let a crab swim into his mouth.
May he plunge in a pool on his way home
   from school
and the current carry him south.

   John Rice

The Poem Imagines it is a Horror Film

He was so afraid that
He had his heart in his mouth.
(*Bloodstains covered his tie*).

It was so funny that
She laughed her head off.
(*They couldn't stitch it back on*).

"Don't look a gift horse in the mouth,"
I was told at school.
(*They bite*).

I hit the nail on the head.
(*It screamed with pain*).

I was so angry
That it made my blood boil.
(*My brains cooked nicely*).

When she lied
I saw right through her.
(*The hole in her head bled*).

My heart sank into my boots.
(*The blood warmed my feet*).

It's not fair –
My teacher keeps
Jumping down my throat.
(*It makes it hard to breeeeeeeathe*).

Pie Corbett

Jabberwocky

'Twas brillig, and the slithy toves
    Did gyre and gimble in the wabe:
All mimsy were the borogoves,
    And the mome raths outgrabe.

'Beware the Jabberwock, my son!
    The jaws that bite, the claws that catch!
Beware the Jubjub bird, and shun
    The frumious Bandersnatch!'

He took his vorpal sword in hand:
    Long time the manxome foe he sought –
So rested he by the Tumtum tree,
    And stood awhile in thought.

And, as in uffish thought he stood,
    The Jabberwock, with eyes of flame,
Came whiffling through the tulgey wood,
    And burbled as it came!

One, two! One, two! And through and through
    The vorpal blade went snicker-snack!
He left it dead, and with its head
    He went galumphing back.

'And hast thou slain the Jabberwock?
    Come to my arms, my beamish boy!
O frabjous day! Callooh! Callay!'
    He chortled in his joy.

'Twas brillig, and the slithy toves
    Did gyre and gimble in the wabe:
All mimsy were the borogoves,
    And the mome raths outgrabe.

Lewis Carroll

From *Through the Looking Glass.*

Walking With My Iguana

I'm walking (I'm walking)
with my iguana (with my iguana).

I'm walking (I'm walking)
with my iguana (with my iguana).

When the temperature rises
to above eighty-five,
my iguana is looking
like he's coming alive.

So we make it to the beach,
my iguana and me,
then he sits on my shoulder
as we stroll by the sea . . .

and I'm walking (I'm walking)
with my iguana (with my iguana).

I'm walking (I'm walking)
with my iguana (with my iguana).

Well if anyone sees us
we're a big surprise,
my iguana and me
on our daily exercise,

till somebody phones
the local police
and says I have an alligator
tied to a leash.

When I'm walking (I'm walking)
with my iguana (with my iguana).

I'm walking (I'm walking)
with my iguana (with my iguana).

It's the spines on his back
that make him look grim,
but he just loves to be tickled
under his chin.

And I know that my iguana
is ready for bed
when he puts on his pyjamas
and lays down his sleepy (Yawn) head.

And I'm walking (I'm walking)
with my iguana (with my iguana).

Still walking (still walking)
with my iguana (with my iguana).

With my iguana . . . .
with my iguana . . . . . .
and my piranha,
and my chihuahua,
and my chinchilla,
and my gorilla,
my caterpillar . . . . .
and I'm walking . . .
with my iguana . . . .

Brian Moses

Mart

Mart was my best friend.
I thought he was great,
but one day he tried to do for me.

I had a hat – a woolly one
and I loved that hat.
It was warm and tight.
My mum had knitted it
and I wore it everywhere.

One day me and Mart were out
and we were standing at a bus-stop
and suddenly
he goes and grabs my hat
and chucked it over the wall.
He thought I was going to go in there
and get it out.
He thought he'd make me do that
because he knew I liked that hat so much
I wouldn't be able to stand being without it.

He was right –
I could hardly bear it.
I was really scared I'd never get it back.
But I never let on.
I never showed it on my face.
I just waited.

'Aren't you going to get your hat?'
he says.
'Your hat's gone,' he says.
'Your hat's over the wall.'
I looked the other way.

But I could still feel on my head
how he had pulled it off.
'Your hat's over the wall,' he says.
I didn't say a thing.

Then the bus came round the corner
at the end of the road.

If I go home without my hat
I'm going to walk through the door
and Mum's going to say,
'Where's your hat?'
and if I say,
'It's over the wall,'
she's going to say,
'What's it doing there?'
and I'm going to say,
'Mart chucked it over,'
and she's going to say,
'Why didn't you go for it?'
and what am I going to say then?
What am I going to say then?

The bus was coming up.
'Aren't you going over for your hat?
There won't be another bus for ages,'
Mart says.
The bus was coming closer.
'You've lost your hat now,'
Mart says.

The bus stopped.
I got on
Mart got on
The bus moved off.

'You've lost your hat,' Mart says.

'You've lost your hat,' Mart says.

Two stops ahead, was ours.
'Are you going indoors without it?' Mart says.
I didn't say a thing.

The bus stopped.

Mart got up
and dashed downstairs.
He'd got off one stop early.
I got off when we got to our stop.

I went home
walked through the door

'Where's your hat?' Mum says.

'Over a wall,' I said.

'What's it doing there?' she says.

'Mart chucked it over there,' I said.

'But you haven't left it there, have you?' she
  says.

'Yes,' I said.

'Well don't you ever come asking me to
make you anything like that again.
You make me tired, you do.'

Later,
I was drinking some orange juice.
The front door-bell rang.
It was Mart.
He had the hat in his hand.
He handed it to me – and went.

I shut the front door –
put on the hat
and walked into the kitchen.
Mum looked up.
'You don't need to wear your hat indoors
  do you?'
she said.
'I will for a bit,' I said.
And I did.

Michael Rosen

Making and Breaking

Oh Emma is my best friend, my best friend,
  my best friend.
Oh Emma is my best friend, the best that there
  can be.
Until she broke me new pen, my new pen,
  my new pen,
Until she broke my new pen,
Now we're not friends you see.

Now Tanya is my best friend, my best friend,
  my best friend.
Now Tanya is my best friend, the best that
  there can be.
Until she beat me test mark, my test mark,
  my test mark.
Until she beat my test mark,
She can't be better than me!

So Meera is my best friend, my best friend,
  my best friend,
So Meera is my best friend, I like her more
you see!
Until she spoke to Tanya, to Tanya, to Tanya,
Until she spoke to Tanya,
She can't do that to me!

But now I have no best friend, no best friend,
  no best friend,
But now I have no best friend, I'm lonely
  as can be.
I think I want to make up, to make up,
  to make up,
I think I want to make up, be friendly with
  all three.
But will they all forgive me? forgive me?
  forgive me?
But will they all forgive me?
I've changed, they'll have to see . . .

Polly Peters

Heartfelt Prayer

In the cold night air
he crouches, sweating,
sweating and praying
that there is a God,
sweating and praying
that there is a God
as he crouches in the cold night air
behind the wall
trying not to breathe,
trying not to breathe
and be invisible
at the same time

please God, don't let them find me
please God, don't let them find me
please God, don't let them find me

Today, there is a God
and he is listening,
listening and answering

and the big boys pass by
muttering as they pass by
Don't worry we'll find him tomorrow
Tomorrow we will find him
Don't worry

And that's all he can do
and that's all he does
in the cold night air,
crouching, sweating,
crouching, sweating and praying
that there is a God,
that there is a God
and he is listening to the prayer
that tomorrow never comes.

But tomorrow always comes,
Tomorrow always comes
And so do the big boys.

Paul Cookson

The Kiss

We'd been flicking through
The Guinness Book of Records
when Joanna found that
the world's longest kiss
had been for seventeen days
in Chicago, U.S. of A.
That's what started the craze
for long-distance kissing.
I kept well away.
Till one day, I was cornered
by the school's professional,
out for a spot of practice –

She said –
'Come on, give us a kiss.'
I said –
'Yuck – NO WAY Hosé!'
She said
'Come on – give us a k i s s s s s s s.'
I said –
'NO WAY – Shirley Whirley,
I'm off.'

So I legged it
to the end of the playground
where she pursued me,
whooping and yelling
like a siren
with lips like suction pads
and octopus arms that made a grab.

So I legged it
to the bicycle sheds
where she followed me
with lips like a frog
and said –
'Come on – give us a snog!'
So I said –
'NO WAY – Not Today,'

So I legged it
to the drinking fountain
where she tracked me down
with a frown
and lips puckered,
ready to kiss me to death.

She said –
'Come on – let's break the record.'
So I thought –
'Euch....mmmmmm.... well.... why not!,
Come on girl – let's give it a whirl!'

Strange then –
that it was she
who scarpered,
quick as a knife,
to the other end of the playground
where she told my best friend,
Petie Fisher,
that I loved her,
and I wanted to marry her
and give her a k i s s s s s s s.

I've decided that kissing
is no good for your health.
I'm keeping my lips
for the nicest person I know.

ME!

Pie Corbett.

Love Poem to Kevin
(HE'D BETTER GET THE MESSAGE!)

Your smile looks like a rip in my jeans,
Your lips resemble an eel,
Your hair has been slurping too much grease,
Can you tell the way that I feel?

Your ears stick up like a pair of forks,
Your hair is greasy spaghetti!
You little squirt of ketchup,
I'd rather SNOG a Yeti!

Andrew Fusek Peters and Polly Peters

We Are Not Alone

When floorboards creak and hinges squeak
When the TV's off but seems to speak
When the moon is full and you hear a shriek
We are not alone.

When the spiders gather beneath your bed
When they colonise the garden shed
When they spin their webs right above your
    head
We are not alone.

When the lights are out and there's no-one
    home
When you're by yourself and you're on your own
When the radiators bubble and groan
We are not alone.

When the shadows lengthen round your wall
When you hear deep breathing in the hall
When you think there's no-one there at all
We are not alone.

When the branches tap on your window pane
When finger twigs scritch scratch again
When something's changed but it looks
  the same
We are not alone.

When the wallpaper is full of eyes
When the toys in the dark all change in size
When anything's a monster in disguise
We are not alone.

You'd better watch out whatever you do
There's something out there looking at you
When you think you are on your own
We are not
We are not
We are not alone.

Paul Cookson

Bogeyman Headmaster

Our headmaster is a bogeyman
Our headmaster is a bogeyman
and he'll catch you if he can.

He creeps through the window
when the school is closed at night
just to give the caretaker a fright.

Our headmaster is a bogeyman
Our headmaster is a bogeyman
and he'll catch you if he can.

When he walks
his feet never touch the ground.
When he talks
his mouth never makes a sound.
That's why assembly is so much fun.

You should see him float through the air
when we say our morning prayer
and at assembly the teachers get trembly
when the piano starts to play on its own.
It's our bogeyman headmaster having a
   bogeyman joke.

Only the lollipop lady doesn't feel scared
'cause when he tried his bogeyman trick
she said, 'Buzz off or I'll hit you with my stick.'

Life can be lonely
for our bogeyman headmaster
but from his office you can always hear
the strange sound of laughter.

   John Agard

The Boneyard Rap

This is the rhythm
of the boneyard rap,
knuckle bones click
and hand bones clap,
finger bones flick
and thigh bones slap
when you're doing the rhythm
of the boneyard rap.

WOOOOOOOOOO!   *(slowly raise arms / hands)*

It's the boneyard rap
and it's a scare.
Give your bones a shake-up
if you dare.
Rattle your teeth
and waggle your jaw
and let's do the boneyard rap
once more.

This is the rhythm
of the boneyard rap,
elbow bones click
and backbones snap,
shoulder bones chink
and toe bones tap
when you're doing the rhythm
of the boneyard rap.

WOOOOOOOOOO!   *(slowly raise arms / hands)*

It's the boneyard rap
and it's a scare.
Give your bones a shake-up
if you dare.
Rattle your teeth
and waggle your jaw
and let's do the boneyard rap
once more.

This is the rhythm
of the boneyard rap,
ankle bones sock
and arm bones flap,
pelvic bones knock
and knee bones zap
when you're doing the rhythm
of the boneyard rap.

WoOOOOOOOOO!   *(slowly raise arms / hands)*

It's the boneyard rap
and it's a scare.
Give your bones a shake-up
if you dare.
Rattle your teeth
and waggle your jaw
and let's do the boneyard rap
once more.

Wes Magee

For Forest

Forest could keep secrets
Forest could keep secrets

Forest tune in every day
to watersound and birdsound,
Forest letting her hair down
to the teeming creeping of her forest-ground.

But Forest don't broadcast her business
no Forest cover her business down
from sky and fast-eye sun,
and when night come
and darkness wrap her like a gown,
Forest is a bad dream woman.

Forest dreaming about mountain
and when earth was young,
Forest dreaming of the caress of gold
Forest rootsing with mysterious Eldorado.

and when howler monkey
wake her up with howl,
Forest just stretch and stir
to a new day of sound.

But coming back to secrets,
Forest could keep secrets
Forest could keep secrets

And we must keep Forest.

Grace Nichols

My Heart's in the Highlands

Farewell to the Highlands, farewell to the North,
The birthplace of valour, the country of worth!
Wherever I wander, wherever I rove,
The hills of the Highlands for ever I love.

My heart's in the Highlands, my heart is
  not here,
My heart's in the Highlands a-chasing the deer,
A-chasing the wild deer, and following the roe –
My heart's in the Highlands wherever I go!

Farewell to the mountains, high-cover'd
  with snow,
Farewell to the straths and green valleys below.
Farewell to the forests and wild-hanging woods,
Farewell to the torrents and loud-pouring floods!

My heart's in the Highlands, my heart is
  not here,
My heart's in the Highlands a-chasing the deer,
A-chasing the wild deer, and following the roe –
My heart's in the Highlands wherever I go!

Robert Burns

How Do I Describe The Snow?

My cousins have asked me
To describe the snow
But I really don't know
How to tell them how
Softly it falls
How gently it fills
Our garden. How wet
It feels after it settles
On my shoulders
How freshly it crunches
Under my heels
How quickly it slides
Down a slippery bank

How thickly it lies
In the school yard
How easily it rolls
Into a ball
How swiftly it
Can shoot away
From my hand

And smash
Against my friend's back
To melt into powder
And be lost in the snow
On the playground!

Bashabi Fraser

The Day the Numbers Spoke

Number one said:
Where I'm going, I go alone.
That is me, myself and I.

Number two said:
I'm part of a perfect couple
and we're heading for the sky.

Number three said:
I've had enough of triangles
O to be a circle for a while.

Number four said:
North, South, East, West, I'm all about,
At home in every direction.

Number five said:
Simply gaze at a single star
and I'll twinkle my reflection.

Number six said:
My fortune takes me far and wide
for I'm the top throw on the dice.

Number seven said:
To the heavens that's where I'll go.
Look no higher than a rainbow.

Number eight said:
I'll slip as snakes intertwined,
A figure of skates in the snow.

Number nine said:
I'll fly with a soul in the night
and the planets wheeling their gems.

Number ten said:
I'm off to meet a dear old friend.
How I long to see zero again.

John Agard

Billy's Coming Back

Word is out on the street tonight,
Billy's coming back.

There's a sound outside of running feet,
somebody, somewhere's switched on the heat,
policemen are beating a swift retreat
now Billy's coming back.

Only last year when he went away
everyone heaved a sigh,
now news is out, and the neighbourhood
is set to blow sky-high.

Words are heard in the staff room,
teachers' faces deepen with gloom,
can't shrug off this feeling of doom
now Billy's coming back.

It was wonderful when he upped and left,
a carnival feeling straightaway,
no looking over shoulders,
each day was a holiday.

And now like a bomb, no one dares to defuse,
time ticks on while kids quake in their shoes
no winners here, you can only lose,
now Billy's coming back.

It's dog eat dog on the street tonight,
it's cat and mouse, Billy's looking for a fight,
so take my advice, keep well out of sight
now Billy's coming back.

Brian Moses

Fight

Call me names, no more games, lay your claims,
FIGHT!
Feel a fool, after school, crowd so cruel,
FIGHT!
Lost my mate, heartbeat rate accelerate,
FIGHT!
Pulling hair, just don't care, no 'there, there',
FIGHT!
Flying fist, fall and twist. Ha! You missed!
FIGHT!
Beat the blues. Blag a bruise., both now lose the
FIGHT!
Same old song with gang along, not right
  but wrong,
FIGHT!
Overdone, setting sun, time to run,
FLIGHT!
Damage deep, wailing weep, will I sleep
TONIGHT?

Andrew Fusek Peters

Dancing Ganapati

Dancing Ganapati, trunk in the air,
we loved you and fed you on milk and sweets,
smeared sandal paste on your marble brow,
decked your pachyderm neck with fresh marigold,
beat on our drums and danced while you stared
with ears fanned out, for we hailed you in joy.
We waved oil lamps and swayed as we sang:
"Dancing Ganapati, trunk in the air,
bless us who worship with milk and sweets."

We slipped away, ate and drank in your name.
Life was as always: flesh-stoned together,
you were our friend, we knew where you stood.
Dancing Ganapati, trunk in the air,
we drank your milk and savoured your sweets
till the day you chose to take our treats –
we wondered where all the milk had gone,
and stared in disbelief at our old playmate:
dancing Ganapati, trunk in the milk!

Debjani Chatterjee

Ganapati is the Hindu elephant-headed god who is
worshipped as the Remover of Obstacles.

For Dilberta

Biggest of the elephants at London Zoo

The walking-whale
of the Earth kingdom – Dilberta.

The one whose waist
your arms won't get around – Dilberta.

The mammoth one whose weight
you pray, won't knock you to the ground.

The one who displays toes
like archway windows,
bringing the pads of her feet down
like giant paperweights
to keep the earth from shifting about.

Dilberta, rippling as she ambles under
the wrinkled tarpaulin of her skin,
casually throwing the arm of her nose,
saying, 'Go on, have a stroke,'

But sometimes, in her mind's eye,
Dilberta gets this idea – She could be a Moth!
Yes, with the wind stirring behind her ears,
she could really fly.

Rising above the boundaries of the paddock,
Making for the dark light of the forest –

Hearing, O once more, the trumpets roar.

Grace Nichols

Dazzledance

I have an eye of silver,
I have and eye of gold,
I have a tongue of reed-grass
and a story to be told.

I have a hand of metal,
I have a hand of clay,
I have two arms of granite
and a song for every day.

I have a foot of damson,
I have a foot of corn,
I have two legs of leaf-stalk
and a dance for every morn.

I have a dream of water,
I have a dream of snow,
I have a thought of wildfire
and a harp-string long and low.

I have an eye of silver,
I have an eye of gold,
I have a tongue of reed-grass
and a story to be told.

John Rice

Words

Words are foods that cannot be eaten, but still
  they feed my mind,
I wallow in the words of wisdom, surprised by
  what I find.
Words together make a sentence; a sentence
  makes a paragraph,
Some words make me angry, some make me
  laugh.
Words are used to hypnotize, put some folks in
  a trance,
Words entwined with rhythm and music makes
  me want to dance.

Words exchanged between two people
If misunderstood could make them fight.
Words used like a key in a lock
Could expose you to the light.
Words speak of different cultures
Their success and their plight.

Some people say I want to be rich
Without money life's a bore,
But! Let me say the more you know of life
The more you feel secure.
Words can help you understand the future
And what's gone on before,
See the book as a stairway
leading you to a door.
Once inside keep searching
Till you reach the core
And if you get lost I'll find your message
Washed up on the shore.

Inside us all, a story waits to take flight,
What I am really trying to say every one of us
    can write.
Write of wars, hatred and peace that's yet to
    come,
Write of people understanding the tongue must
    replace the gun.
Write of your great history, and where you're
    coming from,
Write of nature to which we all belong.

Write of living for today, for tomorrow you
   could be gone,
But if you leave words in a book your legacy
   could carry on.
And maybe your words will inspire the next
   generation
To learn from you and go deeper and then go
   beyond.
So get a pen and some paper sit right down and
   make a start,
No need to worry about the format
Just as long as it comes from the heart.

   Adisa

About the Poets

Adisa

Adisa is a performance poet on a mission to revive the art form of poetry, and take it to the arenas frequented by everyday people. His focus and passion is sharing his words, with the youth of today. Adisa specialises in performing within educational circles and calls his brand of writing and performing VERBALIZM.
Contact: adisa@adisaworld.com

John Agard

John Agard was born in Guyana and came to Britain in 1977. He worked for the Commonwealth Institute as a touring reader, promoting understanding of Caribbean culture. He is an established performance poet and has written several books for adults. His most recent books for children are *Einstein, the Girl Who Hated Maths* and *Hello H_2O* (Hodder).

Valerie Bloom

Valerie Bloom had her first poem published when she was only nineteen years old. She loves to find music and rhythm in poetry and has published a number of poetry collections including; *Duppy Jamboree* (CUP); *Fruits*; *New Baby*; *Selected Poems* (Macmillan).

James Carter

James is a poet and guitarist. He regularly visits schools, libraries and festivals to give poetry and music performances and to conduct poetry writing workshops. *Cars, Stars, Electric Guitars*, his book of children's poems, is published by Walker Books.
Contact: james@94halfpenny.fsnet.co.uk

Debjani Chatterjee

Debjani Chatterjee is one of Britain's best-known South Asian poets. Her recent poetry books for children include; *Animal Antics* (Pennine Press) and with Bashabi Fraser, *Rainbow World: Poems from Many Cultures* (Hodder).
Visit her web site at:
http://mysite.freeserve.com/DebjaniChatterjee

Paul Cookson

Paul Cookson performs poems in schools all over the country as well as editing numerous anthologies. He likes to make people laugh and supports Everton.
Contact: twist@tale.freeserve.co.uk

Bashabi Fraser

Bashabi Fraser is a widely published poet who loves working with children in poetry workshops. Bashabi's recent books include *Rainbow World* (Hodder) which she co-edited and *Tartan and Turban* (Luath Press). Bashabi lives in Edinburgh where she is a university lecturer.
Contact: bashabi.fraser@blueyonder.co.uk

Pie Corbett

Pie Corbett has published over 50 books for children as well as resource books for teachers. He has performed poetry, told stories and taught writing workshops all over Britain.
Contact: pikeorbit@tinyworld.co.uk

Mike Jubb

Mike Jubb is a part-time primary school teacher, who also visits other schools to perform his poetry and to lead writing workshops for children and INSET days for teachers. Apart from poems, Mike has written a children's television comedy drama, several picture books, and a 'toolkit' series for teachers on how to teach poetry at KS2.
Contact: mikejubb69@hotmail.com

Wes Magee

Wes Magee is a former teacher and head teacher who has been a full-time author since 1989. He has published more than 70 books for young readers including poetry, stories, plays and picture books.
Contact: wes@wesmagee.fsnet.co.uk

Brian Moses

Brian Moses writes and edits poetry and picture books as well as writing resources for teachers. He also runs his own poetry and percussion show in schools. A collection of his poems, *I Wish I Could Dine With a Porcupine*, is available from Hodder Wayland.
Contact: redsea@freezone.co.uk

Grace Nichols

Grace Nichols was born in Guyana and moved to Britain in 1977. She has written a number of poetry collections for adults and children. Her children's books are inspired by Guyanese folklore and Amerindian legends and include; *Come into My Tropical Garden*, *Give Yourself a Hug* and *Poet Cat*.

Photograph by Paul Taylor

Polly Peters

Polly Peters is a drama teacher, mother of two
and a fab writer who puts up with her husband,
Andrew Fusek Peters, to write. This unlikely duo
has now written more than 35 books, many
critically acclaimed.

Andrew Fusek Peters

Andrew Fusek Peters is Britain's Tallest Poet. This
requires him to regularly bump into doorways. He
somehow works with his wife on plays, poems,
picture books and a verse novel.
Check them out at www.tallpoet.com

John Rice

John Rice is a poet and storyteller who has
published seven collections of poetry for children.
He regularly performs in schools, libraries and
arts centres. Born and brought up in Scotland, he
now lives in Kent.
Contact: poetjohnrice@hotmail.com or visit his
web site at www.poetjohnrice.com

Photograph by Peter Searle

Michael Rosen

Michael Rosen is known for his unconventional
free-verse and is fascinated by language and the
way we use different words. He has published
many poetry collections including *Michael Rosen's
Book of Nonsense* (Hodder). As well as performing
in schools he is a regular radio broadcaster.

Acknowledgements

All copyright poems reproduced by kind permission of the authors except as follows:

John Agard's 'Keeping Fit' and 'The Day the Numbers Spoke' from *Einstein, the Girl Who Hated Maths* (Hodder Wayland, 2002) and 'Bogeyman Headmaster' by permission of Caroline Sheldon Literary Agency on behalf of the author; James Carter's 'Electric Guitars' from *Cars, Stars, Electric Guitars* © 2002 James Carter, reproduced by permission of Walker Books Ltd; Grace Nichols' 'For Dilberta' © Grace Nichols 1994 and 'For Forest' © Grace Nichols 1988 reproduced with permission of Curtis Brown Ltd, London on behalf of Grace Nichols; Michael Rosen's 'Mart' from *You Tell Me* by Roger McGough and Michael Rosen (1979) by permission of Penguin Books Ltd